I0410076

# MY FINGERS ARE WIGGLING

## Reigning Sunshine series volume 1

Renea Moon

# HELLO POLICE OFFICER

## I HAVE SOMETHING TO SAY...

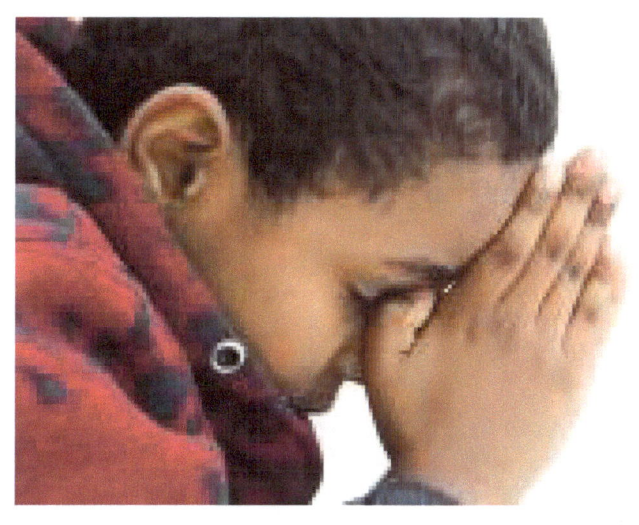

I pray that you always have a good day!

I pray that you always stay out of harm's way.

I pray that you are safe with a wonderful day.

2

# I see you in my neighborhood almost every day.

Some are frightened and scared when you come our way.

They get quiet and leave when you come down the street. They tell us little ones to hurry come in the house and stop dragging our feet.

My mommy sings quietly

while you past us by.

Mommy bends down to

me saying,

"Don't look them in the

eye."

I wipe the corner of my

eyes filled with

water, but I don't cry.

# I do as I am

told and quietly I watch you go by.

Mommy grabs my hand

and holds it real tight.

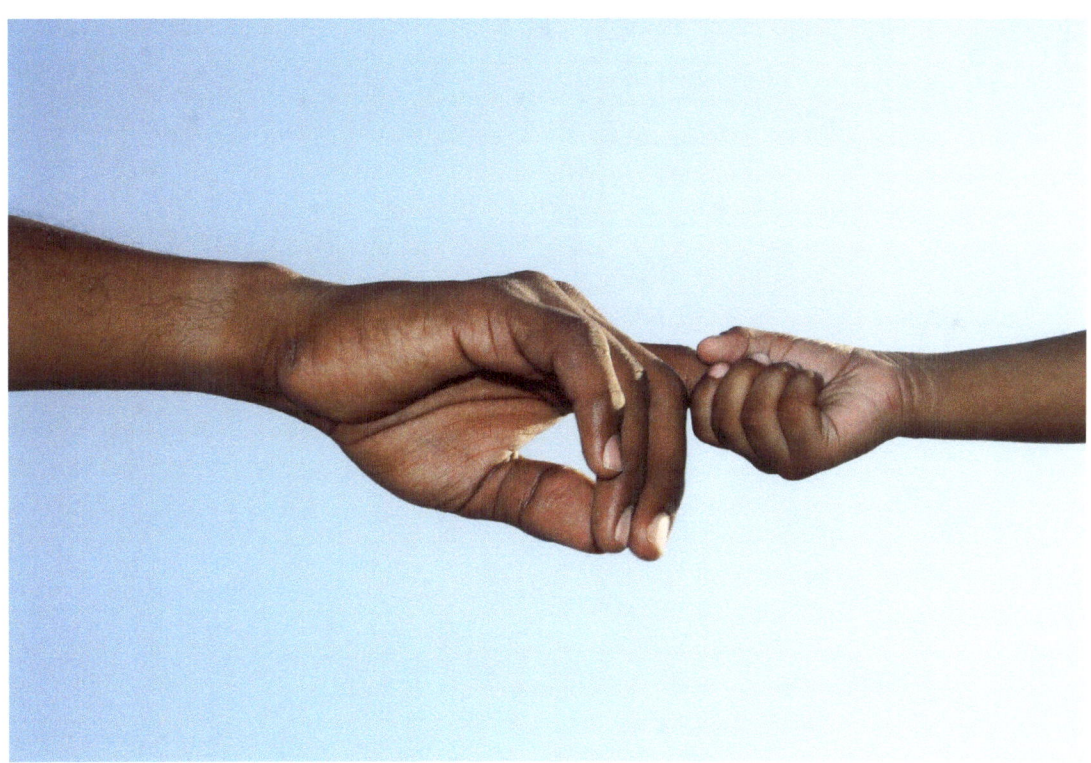

I look up at her

praying softly,

"Lord, please let us all

have a goodnight."

I'm telling you this cause

I want things to change.

Not everyone believes

you can't hear our pain.

I know most of you are

good in the heart and

only want  the best for

everyone and don't

# single us apart.

Yet, I remain faithful

with this to say.

When I got on my knees

and started to pray.

# I got the answer to the

# problem we have...

We should hug it all out

until we  begin to dance,

smile and laugh.

This is something that

we can do too..

We can

hold our hands high

when you come around.

Then we wiggle our

fingers and turn a smile

from a frown.

That's my answer

to what we all should do.

after all God wants us all

to be good thru and

thru...

It's a simple

solution to what we all

need to do.

# My fingers are wiggling

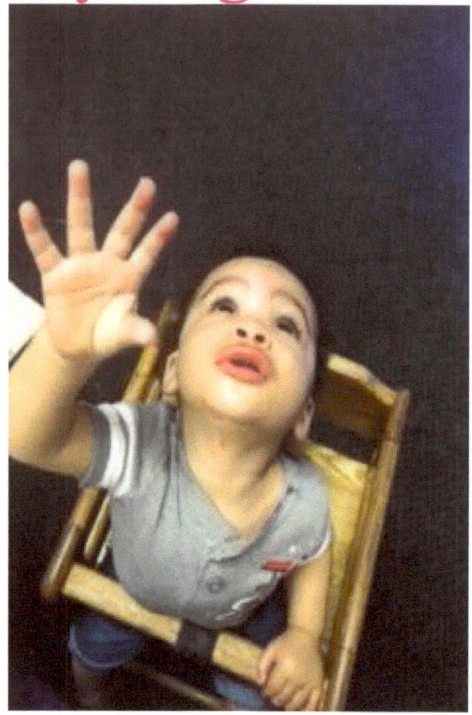

# Mines are too!

That will be our sign...

It will remind you and

me that we are one of a

kind.

# Hello Police Officer, you were a baby like me...

# God created us both to love and to lead...